Short Walks in
The North York Moors

Guide to 20 easy walks

Published by Collins
An imprint of HarperCollins Publishers
Westerhill Road
Bishopbriggs
Glasgow G64 2QT

www.harpercollins.co.uk

First edition 2011
Second edition 2015

Mapping on the inner front cover and all
walking planning maps generated from
Collins Bartholomew digital databases

This product uses map data licensed from Ordnance Survey
© Crown copyright and database rights (2010)
Ordnance Survey (100018598)

Printed in China by RR Donnelley APS Co. Ltd.

ISBN 978 0 00 810157 2
10 9 8 7 6 5 4 3

email: roadcheck@harpercollins.co.uk

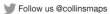 Follow us @collinsmaps

Contents

▶ Short walks

Introduction

Roseberry Topping

Walking in the North York Moors

With a mix of wild moorland, dramatic coastline, rural scenery and historic villages, the North York Moors provides an interesting, and often peaceful region for walkers to explore.

There are about 1400 miles (2200km) of public rights of way within the North York Moors National Park. Copies of definitive maps that show these routes are available for public inspection and are invaluable when deciding controversial sections of little used footpaths.

Following the Countryside and Rights of Way Act 2000 the majority of open moorland, as well as Forestry Commission woodland, is open access land and, with some restrictions this means it can be explored freely on foot. Maps of open access land are available from National Park Centres. Note that all moorland is closed at times of exceptional fire risk and that forestry areas may be closed during felling operations. Landowners also have the right to close their land for limited periods, such as the closure of grouse moors during late May to the end of June when grouse chicks are vulnerable. As with all upland areas the terrain may be difficult and the weather may change quickly so walkers should take particular care when exploring open areas without a well-defined footpath.

Some of the walks described in this guide follow sections of the Cleveland Way, a 109 mile (176km) horseshoe-shaped National Trail that starts at Helmsley and follows the western and northern edges of the North York Moors before reaching the sea at Saltburn and continuing along the coast to Filey. The Cleveland Way opened in 1969 as the second of the long distance National Trails in the UK, and the route is clearly marked with an acorn symbol. Other shorter walking routes are also available. The linking of old tracks and packhorse ways throughout Esk Dale is particularly imaginative and provides walks of varying lengths. Details of these trails and walks are provided on leaflets, issued by the North York Moors National Park, and are usually available from National Park Centres.

The North York Moors Association is an independent charity, established in 1985, that arranges guided walks, talks, visits and other activities to help understanding of the North York Moors. For details of membership and the guided walk programme, see www.north-yorkshire-moors.org.uk or the local press.

Walking is a pastime which can fulfil the needs of everyone. You can adapt it to suit your own preferences and it is one of the healthiest of activities. This guide is for those who just want to walk a few miles. It really doesn't take long to find yourself in some lovely countryside. All the walks are five miles or less so should easily be completed in under three hours. Walking can be anything from an individual pastime to a family stroll, or maybe a group of friends enjoying the fresh air and open spaces of our countryside. There is no need for walking to be competitive and, to get the most from a walk, it shouldn't be regarded simply as a means of covering a given distance in the shortest possible time.

What are the North York Moors?

The North York Moors are one of the largest areas of heather moorland in England. They are bounded to the east by the North Sea, to the north by the Cleveland Hills, to the south by the Vale of Pickering and to the west by the Vale of York. Most of the North York Moors lie within North Yorkshire, with a small northern part of the National Park within the unitary authority of Cleveland.

Man has lived amid these heather moors since prehistoric times. He erected enigmatic stones and cairns, some of which still stand on lonely and windswept heights. With the coming of Christianity, wayside crosses were erected to guide converts physically as well as spiritually. One of these, Ralph's Cross which stands as a lonely roadside sentinel on Rosedale Head, has been adopted as the symbol for the North York Moors National Park.

When the Romans came into the area, they built a road to the coast, which also reached valuable ironstone deposits beyond Wheeldale. They created an early warning system against attack with a series of signal stations along the coast. From early times this length of coast was under threat from seaborne invaders who came, land hungry, from the north-east. This history of surveillance continues with the existence of the RAF Fylingdales radar base on Snod Hill, built in 1962.

Monastic orders found tranquillity and prosperity in the North York Moors. Most of the religious houses, such as Rievaulx, were built in sheltered valleys, but St Hilda chose the wild cliff tops above Whitby.

Following the Norman invasion of England by William the Conqueror in 1066, vast areas of countryside were laid to waste. For a time the North York Moors was almost uninhabited and the castles of Helmsley, Pickering and Scarborough were built to control a conquered land. So few people lived here in the Middle Ages that the moors were used as a royal hunting forest. Favoured religious orders settled or expanded until Henry VIII, in his quarrel with the church, stripped abbeys of their wealth and power. Monks were turned out and magnificent buildings were left to the ravages of the elements. Unwittingly this quarrel led to a new industry that flourished on the coast for several centuries. This was the working of alum between Ravenscar and Guisborough. Used to fix the popular 'turkey red' dyes, alum was a papal monopoly until broken by King Henry.

The movement of goods and salt to the coast, preserved fish inland, and wool and produce to other markets, needed trackways and a complex network of ways developed. Many fine examples of flagged packhorse ways can still be seen in Esk Dale, now linked by a series of waymarked trails. Railways came early with George Stephenson building his line from Whitby through difficult Newton Dale.

Farming patterns have also changed the landscape over the centuries. The tiny subsistencies that followed the breakup of huge monastic sheepwalks and granges have disappeared and large holdings now encroach upon the moors. Plantations of pines have replaced natural woodland cut down as fuel for treating ironstone or alum, and these plantations can be seen on several of the walks in this guide.

Geology

The North York Moors is largely an upland plateau, dissected by streams flowing south in steep sided valleys to the Vale of Pickering. Within this generalisation are hidden some surprising and distinctive landscape features, such as the vast bowl of the Hole of Horcum and the impressive waterfall of Mallyan Spout. It is obvious that the current landscape was created by forces far removed from the relatively gentle climate and watercourses of today.

The dominant rocks in the area were laid down as Jurassic period mudstones and sandstones between 205 and 142 million years ago, when the area was covered in tropical seas. At the beginning of the Jurassic period shales, clays and thin layers of limestone and sandstone were deposited in these shallow waters. A gradual uplifting of the land followed, but there were still times when the current land area was under the sea and this is when marine fossils were deposited. Good examples can be seen along the coast. Fossils found beneath Whitby's east cliff, or on the shore of Robin Hood's Bay, swam or crawled in a sea far removed and warmer than the North Sea of today.

About 2 million years ago a period of glaciation began, ending with the last Ice Age about 20 000 years ago. Towards the end of the last Ice Age the North Sea remained frozen while land ice thawed, and snowfields on the higher land also melted. What is now Esk Dale became a deep lake fed by an ever-increasing volume of water unable to find a seaward exit.

View near Kilburn White Horse

The lake eventually overflowed with cataclysmic force across Goathland Moor to gouge the ravine of Newton Dale. To its south was Lake Pickering, its bed forming the fertile land of the present-day vale, south of the A170 road.

The River Derwent was diverted about the time of this Ice Age. It originally flowed east into the sea above Scarborough, but now flows south through Forge Valley. As part of a flood prevention scheme, a channel known as the Sea Cut was made along the course of the ancient river in the early part of the 19th century.

Distinctive steep hills such as Roseberry Topping, on the northwest escarpment of the moors, were also created as a result of glaciation. They were left partially free of the ice sheet and their present shape was formed by the ice flowing around their flanks.

Wildlife

The varied landscape areas of moorland, woodland and coast support a diversity of wildlife.

Heather dominates on the acid moorland, with the red-purple of bell heather in flower from early July, and the purple of common heather from mid August. Of all the wildlife on the moors the red grouse is the most common. Not a truly wild bird, it nevertheless breeds here, eating the green shoots off young heather until the 'Glorious 12th' of August when the hunting season gets underway. For four months until 10th December, its chances of survival depend upon its ability to dodge the beaters or be missed by an inaccurate shot.

Another moorland sound is the warbling of the curlews on a fine summer's day, an evocative as any sound can possibly be on these windswept heights. The curlew, lapwing and the golden plover may also be seen or heard in the course of a day's walk. Smaller birds such as the skylark and whinchat may make themselves heard but possibly not seen, as also will the wheatear. Moorland birds of prey are the merlin, with its low, rapid flight, the hovering kestrel and the hen harrier, which now visits in winter. On the ground you may spot the rare adder, a much-maligned creature, which prefers to bask in the sun and will only attack under provocation.

With such vast open spaces of moorland it is easy to forget that over a fifth of the National Park is wooded. Much of this is new plantation forest, but there are also areas of native woodland with oak, ash, birch, hazel and hawthorn. These woodlands are often along streams or valley sides where bluebells, wild garlic and anemones bloom in the spring. Daffodils, once an endangered species, are now in abundance, not only in famous Farndale, but also in other quiet areas throughout the southern dales. In the woods and forests there are tits, woodpeckers and finches. Rabbits and hares are in abundance, and you may see that shy woodland dweller, the roe deer.

Along the coast the clay subsoil of the cliff tops is an ideal place for primroses, and yellow celandines are found in marshy places sheltered from the sea. Hazel and other deciduous trees flourish in deep cuttings close to the sea and even manage to survive away from the effect of salt spray behind some of the high cliffs. Blackthorn and furze are the hardiest shrubs, filling exposed hollows in this zone of high winds and salt spray. Numerous colonies of seabirds live around the coastal cliffs where kittiwakes, redshanks and fulmars can be found along with more common species.

North York Moors National Park

In England and Wales, National Parks are areas of outstanding natural beauty where people still live and work. The National Parks and Access to the Countryside Act of 1949 led to the formation of National Parks in England and Wales and the North York Moors National Park was designated in 1952.

The National Park extends over 554 square miles (1434 sq km) and is a roughly kidney-shaped area of heather moor and secluded valleys, ending in the east with the dramatic sea cliffs of the Yorkshire coast. The A170 forms the approximate line of the southern boundary and the escarpments of the Hambleton and Cleveland Hills complete the western and northern boundaries.

The National Park Authority, independent from the county council, controls administration of the Park. The guiding principles of the Authority are both to conserve and enhance the natural beauty and cultural heritage of the National Park, and to promote understanding and enjoyment of the Park by the public. Members of the Authority meet to determine policies and allocate resources.

Most of the land within the Park is in the private ownership of people who live and work there, be they farmers, private landowners or quarry owners. Certain areas of scenic beauty and ancient buildings around the North York Moors are owned by the National Trust, left as gifts by farsighted owners as a means of ensuring their preservation.

One of the statutory functions of a Park Authority is the appointment of full-time and voluntary Park Rangers. These are people with particular knowledge of some aspects of the local environment, who are available to give help and advice to visitors. Other functions of the Ranger service include managing footpaths and bridleways, providing advice and assistance to local farmers in such matters as rebuilding damaged walls to prevent stock from straying, and leading guided walks.

For further information on the Park, and for a greater understanding of the area, visit the two National Park visitor centres. The Moors National Park Centre at Danby Lodge is a former shooting lodge in the Esk Valley set in formal gardens, woodland and riverside meadow. The Sutton Bank National Park Centre, 6 miles (9.5km) east of Thirsk, is at the top of Sutton Bank on the A170 and has fine views west to the Pennines. Both centres provide visitors with an interpretative exhibition of the local environment, film shows and talks, and also offer light refreshments.

Walking tips & guidance

Safety

As with all other outdoor activities, walking is safe provided a few simple commonsense rules are followed:

- Make sure you are fit enough to complete the walk;

- Always try to let others know where you intend going, especially if you are walking alone;

- Be clothed adequately for the weather and always wear suitable footwear;

- Always allow plenty of time for the walk, especially if it is longer or harder than you have done before;

- Whatever the distance you plan to walk, always allow plenty of daylight hours unless you are absolutely certain of the route;

- If mist or bad weather come on unexpectedly, do not panic but instead try to remember the last certain feature which you have passed (road, farm, wood, etc.). Then work out your route from that point on the map but be sure of your route before continuing;

- Do not dislodge stones on the high edges: there may be climbers or other walkers on the lower crags and slopes;

- Unfortunately, accidents can happen even on the easiest of walks. If this should be the case and you need the help of others, make sure that the injured person is safe in a place where no further injury is likely to occur. For example, the injured person should not be left on a steep hillside or in danger from falling rocks. If you have a mobile phone and there is a signal, call for assistance. If, however, you are unable to contact help by mobile and you cannot leave anyone with the injured person, and even if they are conscious, try to leave a written note explaining their injuries and whatever you have done in the way of first aid treatment. Make sure you know exactly where you left them and then go to find assistance. Make your way to a telephone, dial 999 and ask for the police or mountain rescue. Unless the accident has happened within easy access of a road, it is the responsibility of the police to arrange evacuation. Always give accurate directions on how to find the casualty and, if possible, give an indication of the injuries involved;

- When walking in open country, learn to keep an eye on the immediate foreground while you admire the scenery or plan the route ahead. This may sound difficult but will enhance your walking experience;

- It's best to walk at a steady pace, always on the flat of the feet as this is less tiring. Try not to walk directly up or downhill. A zigzag route is a more comfortable way of negotiating a slope. Running directly downhill is a major cause of erosion on popular hillsides;

- When walking along a country road, walk on the right, facing the traffic. The exception to this rule is, when approaching a blind bend, the walker should cross over to the left and so have a clear view and also be seen in both directions;

- Finally, always park your car where it will not cause inconvenience to other road users or prevent a farmer from gaining access to his fields. Take any valuables with you or lock them out of sight in the car.

Equipment

Equipment, including clothing, footwear and rucksacks, is essentially a personal thing and depends on several factors, such as the type of activity planned, the time of year, and weather likely to be encountered.

All too often, a novice walker will spend money on a fashionable jacket but will skimp when it comes to buying footwear or a comfortable rucksack. Blistered and tired feet quickly remove all enjoyment from even the most exciting walk and a poorly balanced rucksack will soon feel as though you are carrying a ton of bricks. Well designed equipment is not only more comfortable but, being better made, it is longer lasting.

Clothing should be adequate for the day. In summer, remember to protect your head and neck, which are particularly vulnerable in a strong sun and use sun screen. Wear light woollen socks and lightweight boots or strong shoes. A spare pullover and waterproofs carried in the rucksack should, however, always be there in case you need them.

Winter wear is a much more serious affair. Remember that once the body starts to lose heat, it becomes much less efficient. Jeans are particularly unsuitable for winter wear and can sometimes even be downright dangerous.

Waterproof clothing is an area where it pays to buy the best you can afford. Make sure that the jacket is loose-fitting, windproof and has a generous hood. Waterproof overtrousers will not only offer complete protection in the rain but they are also windproof. Do not be misled by flimsy nylon 'showerproof' items. Remember, too, that garments made from rubberised or plastic material are heavy to carry and wear and they trap body condensation. Your rucksack should have wide, padded carrying straps for comfort.

It is important to wear boots that fit well or shoes with a good moulded sole – blisters can ruin any walk! Woollen socks are much more comfortable than any other fibre. Your clothes should be comfortable and not likely to catch on twigs and bushes.

It is important to carry a compass, preferably one of the 'Silva' type as well as this guide. A smaller scale map covering a wider area can add to the enjoyment of a walk. Binoculars are not essential but are very useful for spotting distant stiles and give added interest to viewpoints and wildlife. Although none of the walks in this guide venture too far from civilisation, on a hot day even the shortest of walks can lead to dehydration so a bottle of water is advisable.

Finally, a small first aid kit is an invaluable help in coping with cuts and other small injuries.

Public Rights of Way
In 1949, the National Parks and Access to the Countryside Act tidied up the law covering rights of way. Following public consultation, maps were drawn up by the Countryside Authorities of England and Wales to show all the rights of way. Copies of these maps are available for public inspection and are invaluable when trying to resolve doubts over little-used footpaths. Once on the map, the right of way is irrefutable.

Right of way means that anyone may walk freely on a defined footpath or ride a horse or pedal cycle along a public bridleway. No one may interfere with this right and the walker is within his rights if he removes any obstruction along the route, provided that he has not set out purposely with the intention of removing that obstruction. All obstructions should be reported to the local Highways Authority.

In England and Wales rights of way fall into three main categories:

- Public Footpaths – for walkers only;

- Bridleways – for passage on foot, horseback, or bicycle;

- Byways – for all the above and for motorized vehicles

Free access to footpaths and bridleways does mean that certain guidelines should be followed as a courtesy to those who live and work in the area. For example, you should only sit down to picnic where it does not interfere with other walkers or the landowner. All gates must be kept closed to prevent stock from straying and dogs must be kept under close control – usually this is interpreted as meaning that they should be kept on a leash. Motor vehicles must not be driven along a public footpath or bridleway without the landowner's consent.

A farmer can put a docile mature beef bull with a herd of cows or heifers, in a field crossed by a public footpath. Beef bulls such as Herefords (usually brown/red colour) are unlikely to be upset by passers by but dairy bulls, like the black and white Friesian, can be dangerous by nature. It is, therefore, illegal for a farmer to let a dairy bull roam loose in a field open to public access.

The Countryside and Rights of Way Act 2000 (the 'right to roam') allows access on foot to areas of legally defined 'open country' – mountain, moor, downland, heath and registered common land. You will find these areas shaded orange on the maps in this guide. It does not allow freedom to walk anywhere. It also increases protection for Sites of Special Scientific Interest, improves wildlife enforcement legislation and allows better management of Areas of Outstanding Natural Beauty.

North Yorkshire moorland

The Country Code

The Country Code has been designed not as a set of hard and fast rules, although they do have the backing of the law, but as a statement of commonsense. The code is a gentle reminder of how to behave in the countryside. Walkers should walk with the intention of leaving the place exactly as it was before they arrived. There is a saying that a good walker 'leaves only footprints and takes only photographs', which really sums up the code perfectly.

Never walk more than two abreast on a footpath as you will erode more ground by causing an unnatural widening of paths. Also try to avoid the spread of trodden ground around a boggy area. Mud soon cleans off boots but plant life is slow to grow back once it has been worn away.

Have respect for everything in the countryside, be it those beautiful flowers found along the way or a farmer's gate which is difficult to close.

Stone walls were built at a time when labour costs were a fraction of those today and the special skills required to build or repair them have almost disappeared. Never climb over or onto stone walls; always use stiles and gates.

Dogs which chase sheep can cause them to lose their lambs and a farmer is within his rights if he shoots a dog which he believes is worrying his stock.

The moors and woodlands are often tinder dry in summer, so take care not to start a fire. A fire caused by something as simple as a discarded cigarette can burn for weeks, once it gets deep down into the underlying peat.

When walking across fields or enclosed land, make sure that you read the map carefully and avoid trespassing. As a rule, the line of a footpath or right of way, even when it is not clearly defined on the ground, can usually be followed by lining up stiles or gates.

Obviously flowers and plants encountered on a walk should not be taken but left for others passing to enjoy. To use the excuse 'I have only taken a few' is futile. If everyone only took a few the countryside would be devastated. If young wild animals are encountered they should be left well alone. For instance, if a fawn or a deer calf is discovered lying still in the grass it would be wrong to assume that it has been abandoned. Mothers hide their offspring while they go away to graze and browse and return to them at feeding time. If the animals are touched it could mean that they will be abandoned as the human scent might deter the mother from returning to her offspring. Similarly with baby birds, who have not yet mastered flight; they may appear to have been abandoned but often are being watched by their parents who might be waiting for a walker to pass on before coming out to give flight lesson two!

What appear to be harmful snakes should not be killed because firstly the 'snake' could be a slow worm, which looks like a snake but is really a harmless legless lizard, and second, even if it were an adder (they are quite common) it will escape if given the opportunity. Adders are part of the pattern of nature and should not be persecuted. They rarely bite unless they are handled; a foolish act, which is not uncommon; or trodden on, which is rare, as the snakes are usually basking in full view and are very quick to escape.

Map reading

Some people find map reading so easy that they can open a map and immediately relate it to the area of countryside in which they are standing. To others, a map is as unintelligible as ancient Greek! A map is an accurate but flat picture of the three-dimensional features of the countryside. Features such as roads, streams, woodland and buildings are relatively easy to identify, either from their shape or position. Heights, on the other hand, can be difficult to interpret from the single dimension of a map. The Ordnance Survey 1:25,000 mapping used in this guide shows the contours at 5 metre intervals. Summits and spot heights are also shown.

The best way to estimate the angle of a slope, as shown on any map, is to remember that if the contour lines come close together then the slope is steep – the closer together the contours the steeper the slope.

Learn the symbols for features shown on the map and, when starting out on a walk, line up the map with one or more features, which are recognisable both from the map and on the ground. In this way, the map will be correctly positioned relative to the terrain. It should then only be necessary to look from the map towards the footpath or objective of your walk and then make for it! This process is also useful for determining your position at any time during the walk.

Let's take the skill of map reading one stage further: sometimes there are no easily recognisable features nearby: there may be the odd clump of trees and a building or two but none of them can be related exactly to the map. This is a frequent occurrence but there is a simple answer to the problem and this is where the use of a compass comes in. Simply place the map on the ground, or other flat surface, with the compass held gently above the map. Turn the map until the edge is parallel to the line of the compass needle, which should point to the top of the map. Lay the compass on the map and adjust the position of both, making sure that the compass needle still points to the top of the map and is parallel to the edge. By this method, the map is orientated in a north-south alignment. To find your position on the map, look out for prominent features and draw imaginary lines from them down on to the map. Your position is where these lines cross. This method of map reading takes a little practice before you can become proficient but it is worth the effort.

How to use this book

This book contains route maps and descriptions for 20 walks, with areas of interest indicated by symbols (see below). For each walk particular points of interest are denoted by a number both in the text and on the map (where the number appears in a circle). In the text the route instructions are prefixed by a capital letter. We recommend that you read the whole description, including the fact box at the start of each walk, before setting out.

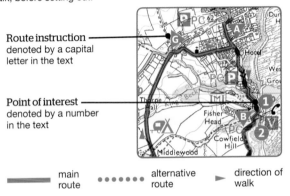

Route instruction denoted by a capital letter in the text

Point of interest denoted by a number in the text

━━━━━ main route   •••••••• alternative route   ▶ direction of walk

Key to walk symbols

At the start of each walk there is a series of symbols that indicate particular areas of interest associated with the route.

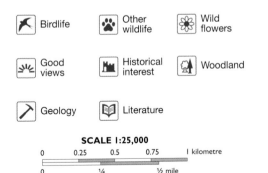

🖾 Birdlife   🐾 Other wildlife   ✿ Wild flowers

🔆 Good views   🏛 Historical interest   🌲 Woodland

⛏ Geology   📖 Literature

SCALE 1:25,000

| 0 | 0.25 | 0.5 | 0.75 | 1 kilometre |

| 0 | ¼ | | ½ mile | |

Please note the scale for walk maps is 1:25,000 unless otherwise stated
North is always at the top of the page

> *A climb to the unmistakable summit of Roseberry Topping, one of Cleveland's most famous landmarks, will reward you with superb views on a fine day*

From the A173 Guisborough to Great Ayton road one can not help noticing the conical bulk of Roseberry Topping, Cleveland's Matterhorn. At 1049ft (320m), it can claim the accolade of being a mountain and looks grand and precipitous no matter how it is viewed. A relic of the Ice Age, its hoary head protruded as a nunatak from the surrounding ice.

Great Ayton is where Captain Cook went to school; the building although rebuilt in 1785, still stands and has been converted into the Captain Cook Schoolroom Museum. In 1934 a house, said to have been owned by Cook's father and therefore assumed to have direct links with the great navigator, was shipped and rebuilt brick by brick by the Australian Government in Melbourne's Fitzroy Gardens. The original site of the house is marked by an obelisk made of stones from Point Hicks where Cook first made his Australian landfall on 20 April, 1770. According to local authority, Cook's connection with the house was, at most, only slight for his father is not supposed to have bought it until Cook was a grown man and away at sea most of the time.

Southeasterly descent from
Roseberry Topping

Captain Cook's Monument & Roseberry Topping

Captain Cook's Monument

Plan your walk

Hartlepool

Middlesbrough

Whitby

Scarborough

Thirsk

Pickering

Norton

York

Selby

Beverley

DISTANCE: 5 miles (8km)

TIME: 3 hours

START/END: NZ574108

TERRAIN: Strenuous; steep section 700ft (213m)

MAPS:
OS Explorer OL 26;
OS Landranger 93

Route instructions

A The walk starts and finishes at Great Ayton station where there is ample car parking. Turn right over the railway bridge then almost immediately right again along a short lane past two or three houses and a chicken farm, into a small field.

B Go left at the junction of cart tracks.

C Turn right on to a lane which soon becomes a path heading towards the lower moors, at first there are hedges on either side then trees later on.

D As the slope eases, look for a yellow arrow and turn left away from the track, aiming uphill by a path

alongside a stone wall to enter the forest at a narrow gate next to a bench. Take the middle of three paths. Bear right steeply uphill crossing a forest track along the way. Continue up a very steep, rough path with occasional steps until it leaves the confines of the pine trees at the top of the rise, to follow a gentler course across the heather moor.

1 The 60ft (18m) high obelisk of Captain Cook's Monument was erected in 1827 by Robert Campion, a Whitby banker. A plaque on the base of the pinnacle tells, in heavy Victorian prose, the story of Cook's epic and brilliant career, which started from fairly

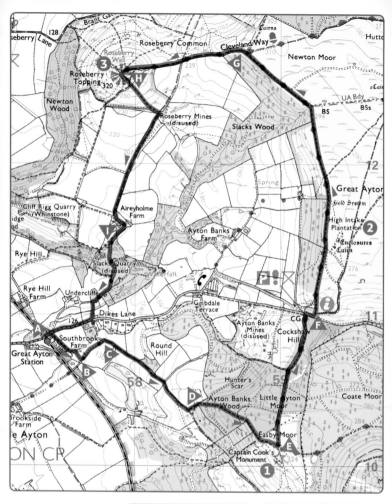

humble beginnings at Marton near Middlesbrough and ended in tragedy on a South Sea island beach after a lifetime of discovery.

From the monument there is one of the finest viewpoints on the North York Moors. Below is the Cleveland Plain with the Pennines stretching as a hazy line from left to right. The bulk of Cross Fell, the Pennines' highest point at 2830ft (893m), and the source of Cleveland's main river, the Tees, can be seen to the northwest on a clear day. Behind the monument a wild vista of moorland stretches into the distance.

Captain Cook's Monument & Roseberry Topping

E Turn left away from the monument and walk downhill on a gradually steepening track, at first through heather and later a pine wood, ending at a picnic site.

F Cross the metalled forest access road at the car park and climb up to the moor by the stepped path. Follow the Cleveland Way signs upwards to the forest boundary wall at the top of the rise. Keep to the right of the wall and along a wide path of springy turf with heather moor on the right. This is Great Ayton Moor, leading to Newton Moor.

2 The proliferation of ancient enclosures, hut circles, cairns and field systems on the moor speaks of habitation in a warmer climate than now. These remains are more evident when there is less vegetation covering the moor.

G Leave Newton Moor and go left through a gate at the angle of the wall. Walk downhill on a well-made path towards the col below Roseberry Topping. Climb the hillside using the zigzag route away from the direct path whenever possible.

3 All of Cleveland is spread beneath the airy peak of Roseberry Topping. Until the 17th century it was called 'Osburye Toppyne' and in troubled times warning beacons were lit on its summit. It warned of the approaching Spanish Armada and later Charles Stuart's rebellious Jacobites. It is a hard climb up, no matter how it is approached but the view from the top will be worth all the effort.

H Walk carefully downhill by a path slanting left below the south side of the summit. Zigzag towards the lower path, through a gate and cross a short section of moorland grazing to join the track to Aireyholme Farm.

I Follow the metalled access lane downhill from the farm as far as the road. Turn right and the railway bridge is about 250yds (228m) away, with the car park approached by steps below a wicket gate on the left.

Roseberry Topping

66 Views of moor and dale, historic castle ruins and
a picturesque pack-horse bridge make this
a walk with much of interest 99

The moors of Ainthorpe Rigg ('rigg' is the local name for a broad
ridge and comes from the Old Norse) were populated in prehistoric
times by a people who have left us a tantalising glimpse of their
technology. Cairns and dykes dot the moor, together with hut
circles and field systems, suggesting that the moors were once
more fertile than today.

Esk Dale, near Danby

Ainthorpe & Danby Castle

Climbing up to Ainthorpe Rigg

Route instructions

Plan your walk

Hartlepool

Middlesbrough

Whitby

Scarborough

Thirsk

Pickering

Norton

York

Selby

Beverley

A The walk starts in the centre of Ainthorpe. Walk south-westwards out of the village, along the Little Fryup road.

B The Fox and Hounds Inn makes a convenient refreshment break, either at the start or finish of the walk. Follow the road uphill beyond the pub towards the open moor.

C Turn right away from the road at the second signposted right of way above a small tennis court and climb out on to the moor along a wide track.

D The path steadily bears left and at the waymark continue straight ahead on to the narrow, but

well-defined path over the heather moor.

1 Viewpoint. Esk Dale winds its way through the moors and Roseberry Topping can be seen as the conical hill in the distance.

2 Viewpoint. Little Fryup Dale is directly below. To the right of the prominent ridge on its far side is Fairy Cross Plain, where legend tells that a young boy once danced around a fairy ring and came under the spell of fairy people.

E Walk down off the moor to the metalled road. Turn left and cross the cattle grid and walk downhill.

DISTANCE: 3¼ miles (5km)

TIME: 1¾ hours

START/END: NZ706082

TERRAIN: Easy

MAPS:
OS Explorer OL 26 & 27;
OS Landranger 94

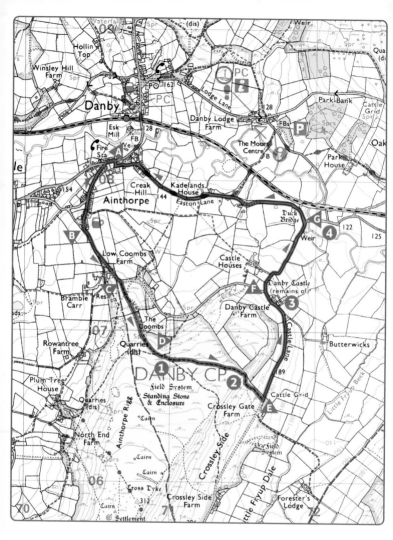

3 Try to visualise the former size of Danby Castle from partly ruined walls beyond the farm house. The former private chamber of the castle was converted into a manorial court house where the Court Leet still meets to administer the centuries old commons grazing system and to settle disputes. The Court Leet rooms can also be hired for private dinners, weddings and corporate events.

Ainthorpe & Danby Castle

Catherine Parr, the sixth and only wife to outlive Henry VIII, would have known Danby Castle; her family owned the castle and lands around it in the 16th century. Now a farm, what remains of the original building speaks of a much grander house.

▶ Turn right at the road junction and walk down towards the river.

④ Duck Bridge is one of the finest examples of a pack-horse bridge in Esk Dale. The name comes from George Duck who restored the bridge in the 18th century. Cars can no longer use the bridge, instead they must cross the River Esk by using the modern ford.

◤ Do not cross the bridge, but turn left along the lane which is followed all the way back to Ainthorpe.

Duck Bridge

> **"** A peaceful walk following a section of the Cleveland Way, and exploring the changed landscape around a once thriving mining community **"**

If you had come into Scugdale about a hundred years ago, you would have found a very different state of affairs to this quiet backwater of today. For a start there would hardly have been a tree standing; the Forestry Commission has planted most of the trees seen today. The biggest impact, however, would have been the number of people round and about, especially on Sundays, when all those engaged in mining were spending their only day above ground. Ironstone mining was an intensive industry both on the edge of Whorlton Moor and in pockets along the valley bottom. Near the start and end of this walk at Huthwaite, lie the spoil heaps of the Marquis of Aislesbury's Scugdale Iron Mine. A light railway from the mine ran across the field beyond the post box - you can still see traces of an embankment.

Scugdale & Live Moor

View from Live Moor

Plan your walk

DISTANCE: 4 miles
(6km)

TIME: 2 hours

START/END: NZ493007

TERRAIN: Moderate

MAPS:
OS Explorer OL 26;
OS Landranger 93

Route instructions

A Park somewhere convenient to Huthwaite Green; usually space is available by the post box. Walk to your right along the Scugdale road as far as the right hand bend beyond Sparrow Hall.

1 Views of upper Scugdale and Whorlton Moor.

B Turn left away from the road on to the easily rising farm track. Walk towards Fog Close Farm, but do not go as far as the farm buildings. Half way up to the farm go through the gate on the right and follow the track to the right through a gate. At the sign turn left and follow the arrows uphill.

C Follow the narrow stream uphill towards the boundary between moor and farmland.

D Go between gate posts in the boundary and bear right out on to the open heather moor. Climb gently uphill avoiding the marshy spot which fills a hollow immediately beyond the gate. The worst parts of a swamp are invariably brightest green, from sphagnum moss which grows only in the wettest places.

E Aim uphill, finding your way on a path through bracken and keeping to the left of the top corner of Snotterdale Plantation. Cross the moorland boundary fence by an easy

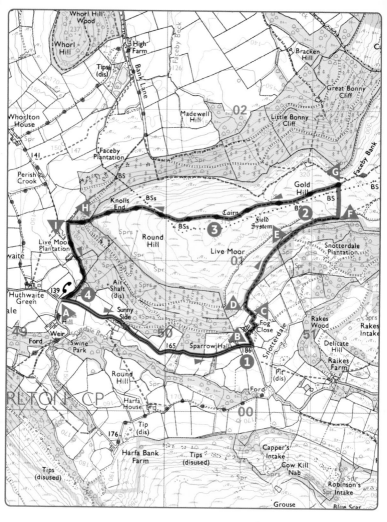

one-step stile and turn right on a wide sandy track.

2 Viewpoint. Whorlton Moor is to the left, the northwestern limit of the Cleveland Hills. Whorlton comes from 'hvirfill', Old Norse for Round Hill.

F As the footpath climbs straight ahead and the track follows the boundary fence to the right, turn left to walk across the open access moorland, keeping the prominent heather-covered mounds to the right. As the marker post for the

Scugdale & Live Moor

Cleveland Way comes into view, head towards it.

G Turn left to follow the Cleveland Way for a little over a mile.

3 From the Cleveland Way there are views of Cleveland and industrial Tees-side stretching from the Pennines in the west to the North Sea in the east. The prominent conical hill in the middle distance to the northeast is Roseberry Topping.

H Go through the gate and walk down the stepped path between two sections of plantation.

I Go left at the bottom of the firebreak to join a bridle-way along the forest edge back to Huthwaite Green.

4 The overgrown spoil heaps on either side of the path are from ironstone mines, once a staple industry of the moors.

Cairn on Live Moor

> **"** This dale is a quiet place and so this walk is one of solitude, through a pastoral valley and then high up on to a lovely old coach road across a windswept heather moor **"**

Bransdale is about as remote as you can get into the depths of the North York Moors. Reached by a narrow unfenced road from Kirkbymoorside and Gillamoor, or an even lonelier one north from Helmsley, the dale shelters beneath the arms of Rudland Rigg and Bilsdale Moor. Forested slopes of Bransdale Moor to the north link the moorland arms to protect this south-facing hollow. Despite its altitude and remoteness, Bransdale manages to smile on the visitor who takes the trouble to explore this Shangri-la of the moors.

Local tales tell of Hodge Hob, a hobgoblin who used to live on the moors above this dale when people were not so sophisticated as they are today. A friendly little chap, he would help in the kitchen or do odd jobs around the farm at night, if the farmer or his wife were kind enough to leave him a spot of bread and milk, but woe betide anyone who crossed him, because all kinds of mischief would then break out. Sadly, Hob and his other goblin friends have gone and we are all poorer by their passing.

Bransdale

St Nicholas Church and Bransdale Lodge

Plan your walk

Hartlepool
Middlesbrough
Whitby
Scarborough
Thirsk
Pickering
Norton
York
Selby
Beverley

DISTANCE: 5 miles (8km)

TIME: 2½ hours

START/END: SE627970

TERRAIN: Moderate / strenuous

MAPS:
OS Explorer OL 26;
OS Landranger 100

Route instructions

A The walk starts by the road junction at Spout House Farm. Try to park well away from the farm buildings and inconvenience no one. Turn left by the farm and walk along the road through the farmyard.

B After about 150 yards (137m) leave the road and turn right and follow the boundary walls of a series of fields.

C Cross the footbridge and follow the main river upstream through another series of fields.

1 Coming upon the substantial group of industrial buildings of Bransdale Mill in a remote corner of Upper Bransdale

is something of a surprise, especially when one takes in their carefully restored state. The mill, owned since 1968 by the National Trust and renovated mainly by the efforts of the Acorn Volunteers, has been here since before the 13th century and is now hostel accommodation. Originally it was a soke mill, an unpopular system which gave the miller a lucrative monopoly to mill corn grown locally or brought into the area. The present buildings are mainly 19th century and date from when it was owned by William Strickland. He changed a simple mill into a complex industrial development. His son Emmanuel Strickland was a man with talents

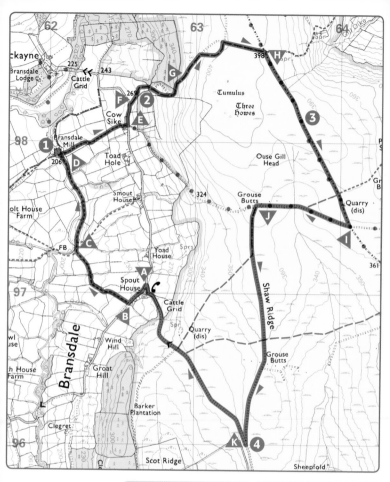

admired in his time; it was Emmanuel who embellished the buildings with classical inscriptions, the most prominent being those on the large plaque above the porch on the east wall. Translated they read as follows:

In Hebrew: Proverbs Ch 1, v 7 *'The fear of the Lord is the beginning of wisdom'*.

In Greek: Thessalonians Ch 5, vv 16 and 17 *'Always rejoice, pray without ceasing, In everything give thanks.'*

In Latin: *'This plaque was set up by me Emmanuel Strickland, B.A. King's College, Cambridge and vicar of Ingleby Greenhow, Cleveland 1837.'*

Bransdale

D Turn right in front of the mill and climb a flight of stone steps to the upper fields. Follow the faint track through the fields as far as the roadside farm of Cow Sike.

E The path skirts round to the left of the farm buildings then left along the road.

F Follow the road into a depression and turn right through a field gate on to a grassy track. Climb towards the edge of the pine forest.

2 Viewpoint. The ancient Bransdale church of St Nicholas fits snugly into the dale head setting, sheltered by the forest from the cold winds that blow down from Bransdale Moor.

G Leave the forest edge to follow a rough track across the moor for a little under ½ mile (805m).

H Turn right on to the sandy moorland road for just under a mile.

3 Here is the old coach road from Kirkbymoorside to Stokesley and Guisborough. Climbing Rudland Rigg to the south it followed a straight course high above the 1000ft (305m) contour for over 8 miles (13km). Humps on the near skyline to the west are the tumuli of Three Howes.

I Turn right on a modern track, used as an access road to the moorland shooting butts.

J Turn left at the track junction. Walk on across the level moor for a mile and then gently downhill towards the road.

4 Viewpoint south along the lower valley of Hodge Beck. Known as Bransdale in its upper reaches, it has three identities before linking with the River Dove and then joining the River Rye, flowing south into the Vale of Pickering.

K Turn right downhill along the road back to Spout House Farm.

Shaw Ridge

" A peaceful route and a pleasing
alternative to some of the better
known areas of the moors "

Fangdale Beck where this walk starts is, like popular
Hutton-le-Hole, a pretty village grouped haphazardly around a
stream, but here the similarity ends. Hutton is all ice cream and
crowds; Fangdale has none of this, no cafés and no gift shops,
and overall there is a quiet tranquillity.

Here is the ideal starting point for a pleasant and varied walk.
Valley paths wander through riverside meadows, which in turn
give way to high pasture, reached by an easy climb beneath
scented pines.

Bilsdale

Fangdale Beck

Plan your walk

Hartlepool

Middlesbrough

Whitby

Scarborough

Thirsk · Pickering

Norton

York

Selby · Beverley

DISTANCE: 4¼ miles (7km)

TIME: 2 hours

START/END: SE569946

TERRAIN: Moderate

MAPS:
OS Explorer OL 26;
OS Landranger 100

Route instructions

A The walk starts in the village of Fangdale Beck, reached from the B1257. Cross the stream and walk up the path towards the converted church. Turn left on to a farm lane.

B Go through the farmyard in front of Malkin Bower Farm, then out along a walled lane.

C At the end of the lane, ignore a prominent path on the left, but turn right through the gate to follow a pathless route around the field, following the signposts.

1 The prominent building across the valley, at the side of the Helmsley road, is the Sun Inn. Next to it is

restored Spout House, a fine example of a 16th-century cruck building. This was an earlier Sun Inn and has been carefully restored to preserve its unique form of architecture. The painting of local huntsmen inside the inn was copied, showing them drinking Bovril, which resulted in the company being successfully sued by the artist.

D Pass in front of Helm House Farm and continue along a track through a series of fields. Where the walled track ends, follow the route by lining up gates as indicated by blue waymark arrows.

E Fork right and climb by forest track, through a

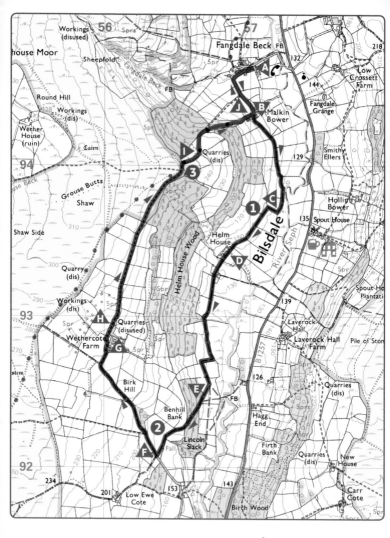

mature pine wood to open
fields above.

2 Viewpoint, south down
Bilsdale looking towards
Ryedale and the forested
slopes of Rievaulx Moor.

F Turn right along the farm
road to Wethercote Farm.

G At the first farm building
on the right, turn left
through the gate into the
field and follow the wall
round to the right.

Bilsdale

At the end of the second field take the gate on the right then turn through another gate on the left. Continue through a series of fields for ¾ mile (1211m) towards open moor. On the moor, keep the edge of the forest in sight about 20yds (18m) to your right.

Turn right through the second gate in the moorland boundary wall and walk downhill along the intake field. Go between two plantations. Sheep and cattle are driven this way out to the moor for summer grazing.

3 Viewpoint. The mass of Bilsdale East Moor rises up on the far side above Bilsdale and the River Seph.

Turn left on regaining the farm lane at Malkin Bower and return to Fangdale Beck.

View across to Bilsdale East Moor

> **❝** This walk is a circuit of Hawnby Hill, but in the three miles it takes to cover the distance, the scenery is a varied composite of everything we can expect to find in this moorland region **❞**

Hawnby Hill itself is a narrow whaleback, not quite, but almost, giving itself mountain status. It was left as an outlier of the moors by the Ice Age, whose retreating glacial tongues honed the hill's north-south alignment and gave it its distinctive shape.

Starting in rich farmland, the route climbs out on to the open moor, before dropping to the headwaters of one of the tributaries of the River Rye. Sad ruins of once prosperous farms dot the sides of Ladhill Beck.

Autumn woodland, Hawnby

Hawnby Hill

Rye Valley

Route instructions

1 Hawnby, with its hospitable inn, is one of those places which has little to offer the tourist who demands gift shops, ice cream parlours and the like, but has much to offer those in search of peace and beauty. It nestles at the southern foot of Hawnby Hill, high above the River Rye. A southward slope away from the village ensures that it gets the maximum sunshine. Sturdy houses built in the warm-coloured local stone complete a charming picture.

A The walk starts in the centre of Hawnby, where there is limited roadside parking. Walk west along the lane past The Inn at Hawnby.

B Turn right at a field gate opposite Manor Farm. Follow a well-defined track through a series of fields.

C Fork right at the junction of tracks.

D Skirt to the right of Hill End House and take the track uphill signposted Moorgate out onto the open moor.

E Cross the moorland road and walk for about 25yds (23m) along the gravel lane opposite and into a shallow depression.

F Cross the stream and turn right away from the lane. Follow a faint path across the heather moor as far as a stile at the junction of two

Plan your walk

DISTANCE: 3 miles (5km)

TIME: 1½ hours

START/END: SE543898

TERRAIN: Moderate

MAPS:
OS Explorer OL 26;
OS Landranger 100

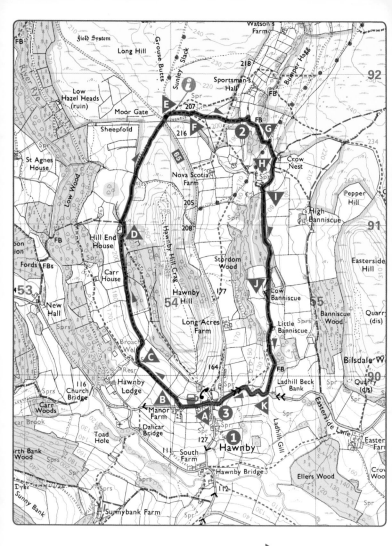

fields with the moorland boundary. Cross the stile into the left of the two fields. Walk downhill towards a copse of scrub birch.

2 Viewpoint of Upper Ryedale.

G Cross the stream at the footbridge. Turn slightly right and walk uphill towards a ruined farm house.

H Go right in front of the ruins of Crow Nest Farm

Hawnby Hill

and descend by an old farm track alongside a field boundary.

▶ Go through the gate into a larch plantation on the gradually improving path, with a soft bed of larch needles underfoot.

▶ Leave the wood for open fields by the track passing the barely noticeable ruins of Low and Little Banniscue Farms.

▶ Turn right at the road. Follow it downhill, over the stream and then climb the short distance back to Hawnby.

3 Viewpoint southwards from the village towards Ryedale.

Hawnby Hill

> **" The highlights of this route are the changing views of the magnificent abbey ruins "**

St Aeldred, third Abbot of Rievaulx, thought of the abbey as a place of peace and serenity and somewhere to escape from the tumult of the world, and if he came back today he would still echo those thoughts. Tucked away in a fold between wooded hills where Ryedale is joined by Nettle Dale, the soaring arches of the ruined windows stand out in majesty amid peaceful surroundings.

This walk is short, but full of interest. The size of the abbey can be appreciated from the number of mounds and walls dotting the fields around, as well as the central ruins. Easy strolling through a meadow leads on to flowery woodland where the soft sound of wood pigeons sets the scene for views of the abbey and terrace.

Rievaulx Abbey

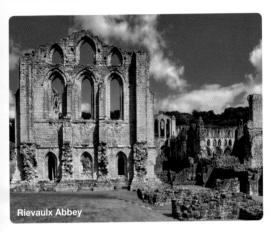

Rievaulx Abbey

Route instructions

Hartlepool
Middlesbrough
Whitby
Scarborough
Thirsk
Pickering
Norton
York
Selby
Beverley

DISTANCE: 2 miles (3km)

TIME: 1 hour

START/END: SE575849

TERRAIN: Easy

MAPS:
OS Explorer OL 26;
OS Landranger 100

A The walk is from Rievaulx Abbey and starts by the car park. Turn right and walk along the road towards the village.

1 Cistercian monks built an abbey here in 1132 and over the years, until 1538, they amassed tremendous wealth from their many lucrative interests. Owning vast areas of land, they were shrewd enough to exploit whatever natural riches came with them. Ironstone, mined on the nearby moors, was smelted into metal for the rapidly expanding economy. Sheep walks covered many miles of moors and salt, produced near the sea, was sold to preserve fish caught by fishermen obliged to give

tithes to the abbey. Rievaulx Abbey is now maintained by English Heritage. The visitor centre includes a museum, exhibition, gift shop and café.

2 Above the abbey is Rievaulx Terrace, an 18th-century pleasure garden laid out in the fashionable style of the time by Thomas Dunscombe. At the northern end of the terrace, a mock Ionic Temple gazes down from its pillared portico above the ruined abbey. A Tuscan Temple to the south complements the idyllic scene. The gardens are owned by the National Trust and the grounds are a riot of wild woodland flowers in spring and summer.

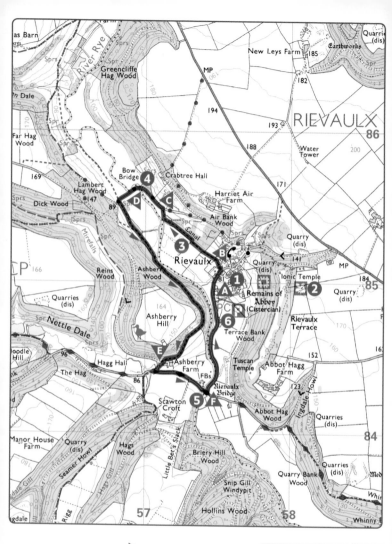

B Turn left away from the road along the path signposted to Bow Bridge.

3 A backward view of the abbey also shows the attractive sandstone cottages of Rievaulx village, some with thatched roofs. The water-filled depression by the path once channeled the abbey water supply.

C Climb up to and through a gate, then turn left into the lane.

Rievaulx Abbey

4 The original Bow Bridge was built in the 12th century but the present day hump-backed pack-horse bridge was built in the mid 18th century.

D Cross the bridge and after 200yds (183m) turn left through a narrow gate. Follow the field track into, then through, Ashberry Wood.

E Go through the farmyard and turn left along the road.

5 Rievaulx Bridge was completed in 1756 to replace an earlier wooden structure that was destroyed by floods. Look over the bridge at the attractive woodland setting of the River Rye.

F Go left at the road junction and along the riverside lane back to the abbey.

6 Fine roadside view of the abbey.

A thatched cottage in Rievaulx village

> 66 A level walk along the escarpment edge to the famous White Horse of Kilburn, enjoying suberb views west to the Pennines and south to York 99

As a walk, with or without the White Horse, there is something for everyone. A level path wanders along the escarpment, and then descends into the forest before climbing back up Roulston Scar. The views are superlative, ranging from the Yorkshire Wolds to the Pennines far away across the Vale of Mowbray; York and its Minster can often be seen to the south.

View from **Sutton Bank**

Kilburn White Horse

View from the Cleveland Way

Route instructions

1 Sutton Bank National Park Centre is an information centre for the North York Moors with displays and interactive exhibitions, gift shop and tearooms.

A From Sutton Bank Car Park, cross the A170 with care. Walk past the viewpoint and follow the level path along the escarpment.

2 Viewpoint with stunning views across the Vale of York below, with the Pennines as a backcloth.

B Continue beyond the plantation.

C Continue ahead, ignoring the path descending to the right and going on past the gliding club field.

3 The narrow path on the right which you will ascend later is known as the 'Thief's Highway', once the escape route of a notorious highwayman who plundered travellers on nearby Hambleton Drove Road. The drove was used by cattle on their way south from Scotland.

4 The path follows the western boundary of The Yorkshire Gliding Club's airfield. Watch the gliders take off and land, but look out for low flying aircraft and falling towlines. The ridge is a perfect setting for gliding, with ideal conditions for hill soaring and few air restrictions.

Plan your walk

DISTANCE: 3 miles (5km)

TIME: 1½ hours

START/END: SE514830

TERRAIN: Easy

MAPS:
OS Explorer OL 26;
OS Landranger 100

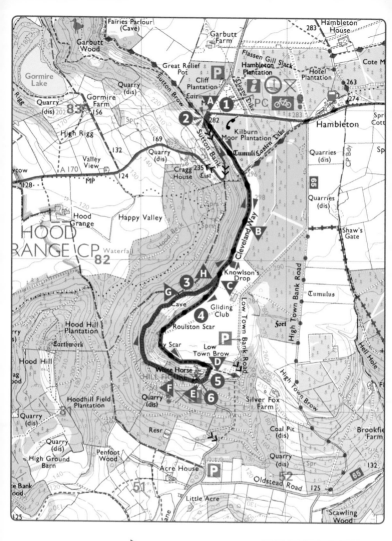

▶ Follow the path above the White Horse. Turn right beyond its 'tail' and walk down a flight of steps as far as the car park.

5 Viewpoint. The White Horse is below. Please do not walk on it, but keep to the path and prevent erosion. Beyond, across the Vale of Pickering, are the Pennines and on a clear day you may see York Minster 18 miles (29km) away.

Kilburn White Horse

6 Kilburn White Horse was dug by children from Kilburn school in 1857 under the direction of their schoolmaster, John Hodgson, and its designer, Thomas Taylor. Although designed at 314ft (96m) long and 228ft (70m) high it is now 318ft (97m) long and 220ft (67m) high, and in surface area it is Britain's largest white horse. The structure is regularly maintained by the Kilburn White Horse Association.

E Turn right and go through a gate at the corner of the car park to follow the forest path straight ahead.

F Bear right where the track forks and follow the path below the cliffs.

G Where the track forks, bear right steeply uphill.

H At the top of the hill, turn left to follow the outward path along the escarpment back to Sutton Bank.

Kilburn White Horse

❝ A remote walk through forest and farmland ❞

HELMSLEY
2½ miles

The road north from Helmsley to Bransdale must be about the quietest road on the North York Moors. Once it leaves the hamlet of Carlton, the road is the only link with the outside world for a scattering of remote hill farms and forestry workers' homes. Even the chance of meeting other walkers is less likely here than most other routes in the North York Moors.

Footpath sign at Carlton

Upper Riccal Dale

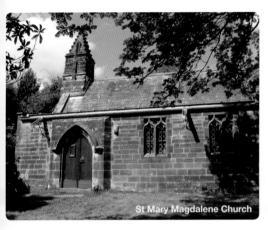
St Mary Magdalene Church

Hartlepool
Middlesbrough
Whitby
Scarborough
Thirsk
Pickering
Norton
York
Selby
Beverley

Route instructions

A Leave the car in the scenic car park at the top of Cowhouse Bank. Follow the forest track southeast over the road into Riccal Dale Wood.

B Turn left at the junction of tracks and walk downhill through the plantations of pine forest.

C Turn left at the junction with a forest drive.

D Go right on joining a farm road. Cross the bridge and climb through two fields away from the stream towards Howl Wood Farm. Notice the herculean efforts of previous farmers who built boundary walls from massive boulders cleared from the fields.

E Go left through the farmyard and left through a gate beyond the farm tip to follow a faint track ahead, bearing left at a track junction.

F Cross the stream by the footbridge.

G Follow the path uphill beyond the stream then bear left, then right into a field keeping the boundary close by on the right. Cut across an area of rough grazing and walk towards the road, aiming to the left of the forest chapel.

H Cross the metalled road and go on to a forest road.

1 The small church of St Mary Magdalene lies

DISTANCE: 5 miles (8km)

TIME: 2½ hours

START/END: SE612887

TERRAIN: Moderate

MAPS: OS Explorer OL 26; OS Landranger 100

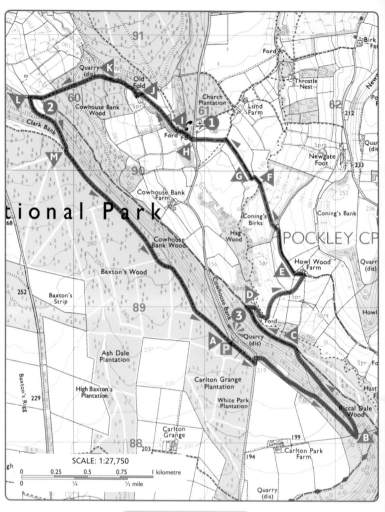

tucked amongst the surrounding pines trees. The area once had a population of over 200 but the church now serves a small community scattered over many miles of moor and forest.

▶ **I** Cross the footbridge by the side of the ford. Walk upstream straight ahead.

▶ **J** Follow the garden wall of the farmhouse, first to the left and then right to join a forest track.

▶ **K** Continue ahead on the forest track.

Upper Riccal Dale

▶ At the open field, turn left away from the track on a path between forest and the field's upper boundary.

2 From Clark Bank viewpoint you can see Bilsdale Moor to the north. The word 'Bank' is a local term for a steep slope, usually with an access track.

▶ At the top of the bank, turn left along the forest bridleway. Follow this level track for 1¼ miles (2 km) all the way back to Cowhouse Bank car park.

3 Cowhouse Bank viewpoint has stunning views across Bransdale, and a convenient seat to enjoy them on.

View from Cowhouse Bank

❝ A gentle walk along farmland
paths and country lanes between two of
North Yorkshire's most attractive villages **❞**

Hutton-le-Hole is one of North Yorkshire's most popular villages.
The houses are scattered at random around its green and Hutton
Beck tumbles through their midst in a series of short waterfalls.
Sheep graze on either side of the unfenced road to complete a
scene that has been featured on many calendars and in countless
photographs. Lastingham is not so well-known as Hutton-le-Hole,
but is arguably more attractive with old houses grouped together
along two streets. Both places are fine examples of moorland
villages with traditional stone cottages roofed in red pantiles.

Hutton-le-Hole

Hutton-le-Hole

Route instructions

1 The imaginative open-air Ryedale Folk Museum has been developed to cover 3 acres (1.2ha) on one side of the main street of Hutton-le-Hole. Local antiques and crafts are on display in the open air or in restored farm buildings, some of which have been moved here from places throughout the moors.

A From the car park, walk down to the Ryedale Folk Museum and then go past the chapel. Turn left at a footpath sign and keep to the left of the bowling green. Cross a series of fields and Fairy Call Beck.

B Turn right on the road and walk along its wide grassy verge.

C Where the road bends sharply right, turn left away from it on to a rough track for about 120yds (110m) at the side of a swampy field to a path junction.

D Fork right following a well-defined path out on to the open moor. Keep the field boundary wall in sight a few yards to your right and walk as far as the group of buildings of Camomile Farm. Turn left away from the farm, still following the boundary, to cross a small but steep-sided valley.

E Turn right at a footpath junction to join the lane into Lastingham village.

2 There was a Benedictine Abbey at Lastingham, built

Plan your walk

Hartlepool

Middlesbrough

Whitby

Scarborough

Thirsk

Pickering

Norton

York

Selby

Beverley

DISTANCE: 4 miles (6km)

TIME: 2 hours

START/END: SE705902

TERRAIN: Easy

MAPS:
OS Explorer OL 26;
OS Landranger 100

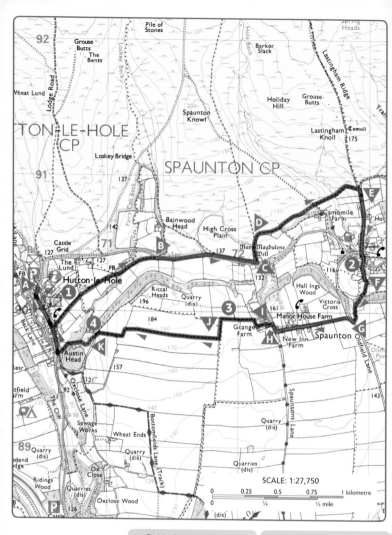

on Celtic foundations, but it was destroyed by the Danes in 862. It lay in ruins until monks from Whitby temporarily re-established it in 1078, before moving to York in 1086. They left a fine Norman crypt, which is under the present church.

There are two irreverent stories connected with this church. One is that a vicar used a carved oak server as firewood to melt lead from the church roof. The other concerns the crypt, which was used for cockfighting in the 18th century.

Hutton-le-Hole

F Pass a row of riverside cottages, fork right beyond the last one and walk up the steep grassy track. The track can be muddy after rain, but with a little care the worst parts can be avoided.

G Climb through a belt of mature beech trees as far as the road. Bear right and walk through Spaunton.

H Turn right at the T-junction and then left to Grange Farm.

I Follow direction signs through the farmyard.

3 Viewpoint. Spaunton Moor and Blakey Ridge, a blaze of colour in the autumn, climbs in rolling waves beyond the intervening valley.

J Follow a waymarked path around the edge of a series of fields.

4 From here there is a good view of Hutton-le-Hole.

K Go downhill through sparse woodland to the roadside. Hutton village is on the right.

Lastingham

In spring the daffodils rival those of Farndale, but are not so well known and therefore not visited by the same number of people. Autumn sees the moors change to a rich purple when the scent of heather can be almost overpowering. Summer is when the high meadows are ready for haymaking and it is then that the field flowers are at their best. Winter, in its turn, brings frost and snow and a grand silence between the storms, when nature tempts the unwary out on to the moors.

The valley prospered when ironstone was mined, but with the decline of the industry it has moved back to being a sleepy backwater. Once-polluted streams now sparkle again and forest plantations cloak the hillside, replacing trees cut down to fuel medieval iron furnaces.

Moorland above Rosedale Abbey

Rosedale Abbey

View across North Dale

Route instructions

1 Apart from a wall and the ruin of a tower, all that remains of Rosedale Abbey has been incorporated into Rosedale parish church. Built for Cistercian nuns in 1158 by William of Rosedale, it lasted until 1536 when the edict of Henry VIII spelt its end. The abbey had its own sacred well, which can be found inside a low stone shelter standing at the entrance to the nearby campsite. The Rosedale Circuit, a tough 37 mile (59.5km) walk which crosses nine dales and involves about 5000ft (1524m) of climbing, starts and finishes at Rosedale Abbey.

A The walk starts in the centre of Rosedale Abbey village. Turn right between the car park and a converted chapel, then bear left uphill to start walking upstream through a series of meadows, crossing field boundaries by stiles or gates for just under 1 mile (1.6km).

B Aim uphill towards the ruined barn. Before the wooden footbridge turn right uphill keeping the stone wall on the left. Before you reach the barn turn left through a gate, then diagonally right through the next gate. Bear left, keeping to the right of the field boundary.

C Join the farm road, then turn right and walk as far as a group of farm buildings alongside the road.

Plan your walk

Hartlepool
Middlesbrough
Whitby
Scarborough
Thirsk
Pickering
Norton
York
Selby
Beverley

DISTANCE: 4¼ miles (7km)

TIME: 2¼ hours

START/END: SE705960

TERRAIN: Moderate

MAPS:
OS Explorer OL 26;
OS Landranger 100

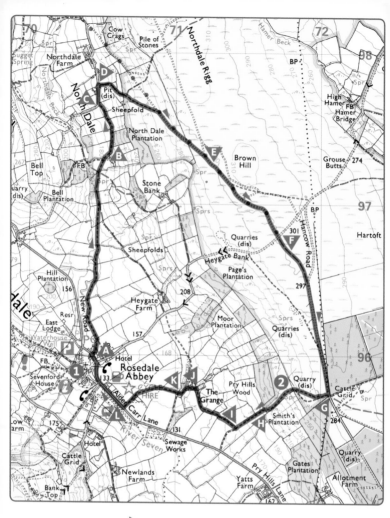

D Turn right at the end of the barn on the right of the road. Follow the signposted bridleway uphill towards the open moor. At the gate at the top of the field bear right following the footpath sign.

E Walk ahead to join a moorland track coming from the left. Keep right at the next fork and aim for the road which will be indicated by passing cars.

F Cross the road and follow the direction of a signpost pointing the way through the heather. The path is narrow and if you

Rosedale Abbey

are in any doubt, keep slightly to the left towards the upper road as shown on the map. Turn right on the road and follow it as far as a cattle grid by the forest edge.

G Turn right away from the road at the cattle grid. Go downhill across the rough moor away from the pine forest. Walk towards the near corner of the small plantation lower down the hillside; the plantation will not be immediately apparent.

2 Viewpoint. Rosedale is in the foreground, with Blakey Ridge filling the skyline.

H Cross the stile and continue downhill through the lower field alongside a boundary wall to a path junction.

I Turn right across two adjoining stiles and follow yellow waymark arrows towards The Grange Farm. After rain there may be mud in the immediate vicinity of the farmyard.

J Keep left through the farmyard and down to a ford.

K After the ford turn right and follow a signposted route over two fields keeping to the right of the buildings close to the road ahead. Go to the right of the house, then walk down the drive to the road.

L Turn right and follow the road back to Rosedale Abbey.

View across Rosedale to Blakey Ridge

" A scenic walk exploring sections of the beautiful dales of Newton and Dalby, and linking them with the smaller ones of Cross and Levisham **"**

The walk takes us down through Levisham Dale, the first of the four dales, then into Newton Dale where steam trains thread their way from Pickering to Grosmont and Whitby. A short but steep climb up Cross Dale and a stretch of farmland and forest on either side of the A169 leads to Dalby Dale.

Steam train leaving Levisham station, North Yorkshire Moors Railway line

Lockton – Four Dales Walk

Well commemoration plaque

Hartlepool

Middlesbrough

Whitby

Scarborough

Thirsk

Pickering

Norton

York

Selby

Beverley

DISTANCE: 5 miles
(8km)

TIME: 3 hours

START/END: SE844900

TERRAIN: Moderate;
one steep uphill section
426 feet (130m)

MAPS:
OS Explorer OL 27;
OS Landranger 100

Route instructions

A The walk starts by Lockton Church. Walk westwards along the village street ignoring the Levisham turning. Take the narrow signposted footpath straight ahead and then right at the end of the road.

1 Lockton is a pleasant little village just far enough away from the busy A169 to be unaffected by its traffic. Medieval St Giles' Church is simple in style, with a notable stained glass window, and is a fine example of an ancient country church. A plaque tucked away on the side of a house on the left, below the church, commemorates the building of a well in 1697. The names of eight benefactors were recorded,

but one has obviously been removed; does this hide a local quarrel, or simply an error? Water is still a valuable commodity on this dry upland plateau and today it has to be pumped to a storage tank.

B Go left along Levisham Dale crest.

2 This viewpoint down into the dale is partly obscured by trees but it is still possible to see the top of the tiny church of St Mary's which once served Levisham. There was once a thriving community living around a mill in the valley bottom.

C Follow the zigzag path downhill into Newton Dale.

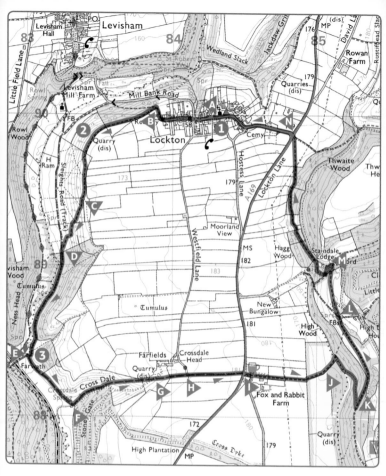

D Turn left on a bridle path heading down towards woodland.

E At a footpath junction turn left to cross a narrow field below the woodland boundary.

3 This is a good place to watch steam trains below in Newton Dale. The 18 mile (29km) North Yorkshire

Moors Railway is a well-preserved and very popular heritage railway. The line was first opened in 1836 as the Whitby and Pickering Railway to open up trade inland from Whitby. It became uneconomic and closed in 1965 before re-opening in 1973 to eventually become a major tourist attraction, carrying more passengers than

Lockton – Four Dales Walk

any other heritage railway in the UK.

F Climb steeply to the left up the dry valley of Cross Dale.

G Keep to the right of the farm at the valley head and aim towards a walled track.

H Join a farm lane and walk on to the main road.

I Cross the road and follow footpath signs between the Fox and Rabbit Farm buildings. Walk away from the farm by the path, as indicated by signs around the field boundaries.

J Continue straight ahead into woodland and when a footpath is signposted off to the left, ignore it and follow the path going right crossing a wall into further forest. Walk along the fire break and after a couple of minutes turn hard left into Dalby Dale.

K Go to the left and away from the driveway to Staindale Lodge. Prior to entering woodland, turn right on to the footpath signposted to Lockton. Follow the path, eventually climbing beyond the trees, then between a series of fields as far as the main road.

L Cross over the forestry road and follow the river bank upstream.

M Go left in front of the main building of Staindale Lodge. Follow the driveway uphill. Just before woodland, turn right onto the footpath signposted Lockton. Follow the path to climb beyond the trees, then between a series of fields as far as the main road.

N Cross the road with care and walk down the lane opposite to Lockton.

Levisham Dale

> Starting from a popular viewpoint over the natural amphitheatre of the Hole of Horcum, this walk follows ancient tracks offering other vantage points with far-ranging views

The pressures of intensive farming and forest planting on the natural moorland are highlighted on this walk. A short and easy walk, but one which is marked by contrasts, be they the view of the deep Hole of Horcum or the sharp edge of mature forest on Blakey Rigg to the north east. Two ancient tracks are used and both keep to the edge of high escarpments. The purpose of these old ways was to take salt to the coast and preserved fish back inland. Saltergate Brow, between Gallows Dike, above the Hole of Horcum, and Whinny Nab, indicates its previous use but the name of Old Wife's Way is more elusive.

Whinny Nab

Hole of Horcum

Route instructions

1 The deep natural hollow of the Hole of Horcum opens up beyond the road. Local legend tells that it was created by a giant who scooped up the rock and soil and used it to create Blakey Topping.

A Leave the Saltergate Bank car park and walk to the right a little way along the main road as far as the farm lane on the right. Turn into it to follow the lane alongside flat, intensively-farmed fields for a little under 1 mile (1.6km).

2 The Old Wife's Way is an ancient pack horse track. Who the Old Wife was has never been recorded. It is possible that she was a tinker woman, who sold her small but essential trinkets and ribbons to farmers' wives across the moor. Another theory is that the she was an earth mother or goddess associated with moorland fertility rites thousands of years ago.

B Turn left at the junction and walk steeply downhill on the concrete track to Newgate Foot Farm.

3 The land falls steeply into Long Gill, a deep defile scoured by overflowing melt water at the end of the last Ice Age. Beyond, Blakey Topping stands above Allerston and Langdale Forests.

C As the track approaches the farmyard turn left

Plan your walk

DISTANCE: 3½ miles (5.5km)

TIME: 1¾ hours

START/END: SE853937

TERRAIN: Easy

MAPS:
OS Explorer OL 27;
OS Landranger 100 & 101

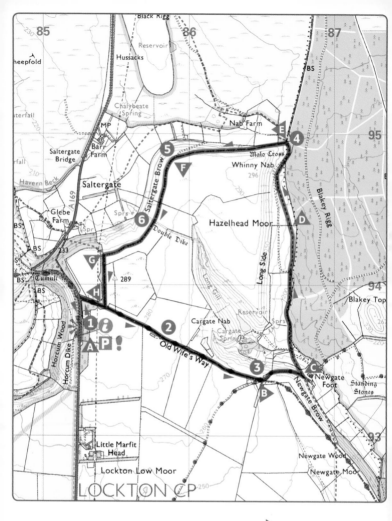

through a gate at the top of some steps and follow a signposted footpath downhill to the left. Head for the valley floor, passing through several gates. There is no obvious footpath, but the right of way aims towards the forest edge and follows it to Whinny Nab.

▷ After the last field cross the stile into open moorland.

4 Malo Cross is an ancient way mark on the salt way to Whitby. The view to the north is of Fylingdales Moor and the complex radar equipment of the Ministry of Defence.

Whinny Nab

E Turn left at the cross and gently climb the side of Whinny Nab by a bridle track signposted to Horcum.

F The bridleway climbs the gentle slopes of Saltergate Brow. Furze and scrub trees line the edge of this escarpment and sheep browse to the south.

5 The view here is across Fen Moor and the deep trough of Newton Dale with Wheeldale Moor beyond.

6 Twin furrows mark the line of Double Dike, a Bronze Age boundary that links Long Gill to the escarpment of Saltergate Brow.

G Turn left at the shelter belt of fir trees and walk with them on your right and sheep pasture to the left.

H Join the farm road of Old Wife's Way and turn right to walk to the main A169. Turn left and walk a short way back to the car park.

Blakey Topping

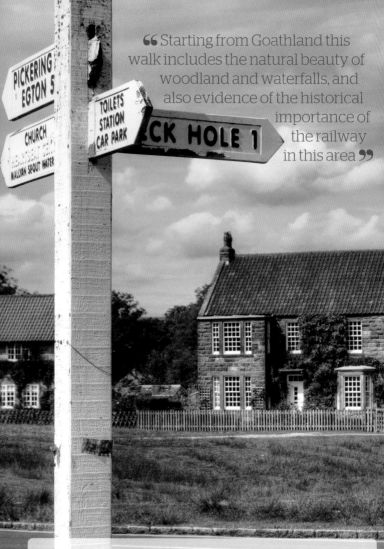

" Starting from Goathland this walk includes the natural beauty of woodland and waterfalls, and also evidence of the historical importance of the railway in this area **"**

PICKERING
EGTON 5

TOILETS
STATION
CAR PARK

CHURCH

MALLYAN SPOUT WATER

CK HOLE 1

Goathland is perhaps best known as the location for Aidensfield in the successful TV series Heartbeat. The main village straggles along the road above Eller Beck, but the upper village is clustered around its open common, where grazing sheep come right up to cottage doors.

Village signpost in Goathland

Mallyan Spout & Goathland

Goathland Hotel

Route instructions

1 The railway was first opened to horse-drawn trains in 1836, when George Stephenson laid a track from Whitby to Pickering, south of Grosmont. Technical problems meant that the line had to climb high above the river in the space of three miles. The only way to climb the 197ft (60m) to Goathland was to haul rolling stock by a rope, up the 1 in 15 incline from Beck Hole. Despite modifications, the line was unsatisfactory and in 1865 a 'Deviation Line', was blasted through solid rock along the present route now used by the North Yorkshire Moors Railway.

A Park on the upper car park and then turn right

along the lane, then left for about 180 yards (165m).

B Turn right at the Goathland Hotel and walk along the cinder track of the old railway.

C Turn right at Abbot's House Camp Site and follow the signposted path through two fields. Cross a small stream by the footbridge and walk through a series of fields alongside a plantation of mature pines.

D Cross the common to the Mallyan Spout Hotel. Take the signposted path downhill to the right of the hotel. Follow it through a narrow belt of trees into the wooded valley. Note that

Plan your walk

DISTANCE: 3½ miles (5.5km)

TIME: 1¾ hours

START/END: NZ834014

TERRAIN: Easy

MAPS:
OS Explorer OL 27;
OS Landranger 94

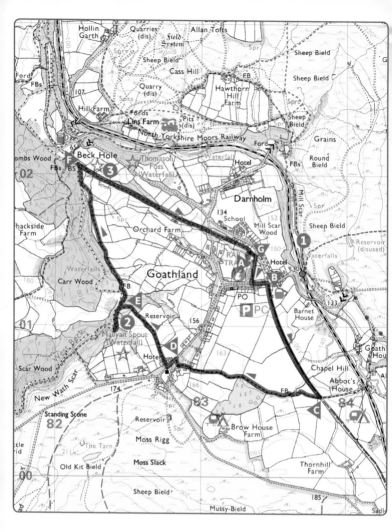

this is a popular footpath that can be very muddy and slippery after rain.

E Turn left at the river to reach Mallyan Spout. Return to this point afterwards; the walk continues downstream on a clearly defined footpath,

crossing field boundaries through gates and following the edge of the wooded ravine of West Beck.

2 At 70ft (21m) high, Mallyan Spout is the tallest waterfall in the North York Moors and is at its most

Mallyan Spout & Goathland

impressive after a period of wet weather. The path to the waterfall is over smooth boulders and is often slippery.

F Turn right at Incline Cottage and climb the tree-lined cinder bed of the incline to walk along the route of the dismantled railway.

3 Coaches and wagons were hauled up this incline by a rope. Notice the attractive architecture of the track-side cottages at Beck Hole and also at the top of the incline. There is a short piece of the original iron rail on its stone block sleepers, outside Incline Cottage at Beck Hole.

G Turn right at the top of the incline on the road back to the car park.

Mallyan Spout

> **" Follow shady woodland paths along the valley bottom, then climb the valley side to find rolling acres of farmland filling the plateau above "**

Here is nature's engineering on the grand scale. The deeply wooded gorge of Forge Valley is the 'unnatural' route of the Derwent, its original course being that now used by the flood prevention scheme known as the Sea Cut, which follows a wide valley bottom in a direct line to the sea. Towards the end of the last Ice Age, when the still frozen North Sea held back melt waters from the land, the Derwent had nowhere to go other than through a narrow side valley to the south. Such was the volume of water flowing through this minor valley that it deepened and when the sea eventually thawed, the river continued on its new course, flooding what is now the Vale of Pickering. The Sea Cut, dug in the mid 19th century, reduced the danger of flooding and greatly improved land in the vale.

Forge Valley National Nature Reserve

Forge Valley

Forge Valley

Route instructions

A Leave the car in the scenic car park at Green Gate and walk south downstream along the road in the direction of East Ayton, following the river for about a quarter of a mile (0.5km).

1 Forge Valley Woods have been designated a National Nature Reserve to conserve their natural beauty. The trees are mostly deciduous, growing on an alkaline soil based on the underlying oolitic limestone. Woodland flowers, such as anemones, bluebells and primroses, flourish in their season, and on the riverbanks the marsh marigolds are beautiful in late spring. The woods were once coppiced to provide charcoal for the forge that gave the valley its name.

B Turn left at the footpath sign, away from the road and walk uphill beneath beech and other limestone loving trees. Keep on heading in about the same direction, ignoring any paths that turn sharp right or left. As the path descends to the road immediately take the next path uphill to the left.

2 Rock was quarried here for lime and building stone. Warm hues in the quarry face are of oolite, a fine-grained limestone laid down in a shallow coral sea during the Jurassic period 160 million years ago. The name 'oolite' comes from the Greek word for fish roe.

Plan your walk

Hartlepool
Middlesbrough
Whitby
Scarborough
Thirsk
Pickering
Norton
York
Selby
Beverley

DISTANCE: 3½ miles (5.5km)

TIME: 1¾ hours

START/END: SE984875

TERRAIN: Moderate

MAPS:
OS Explorer OL 27;
OS Landranger 101

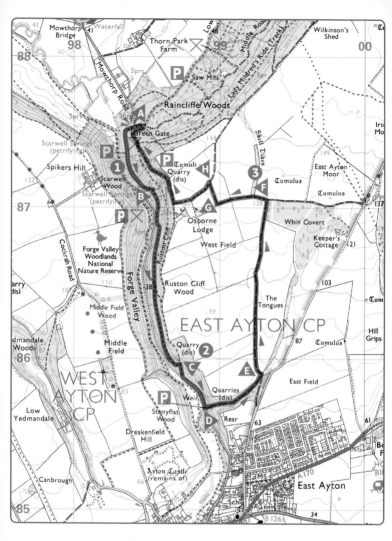

C From the quarry follow the path downhill to rejoin the road.

D Turn left at the footpath sign and climb away from the road, through woodland on a wide path giving easy access to the open plateau above.

E At the junction of field tracks, turn sharp left on to a sunken track, following it as far as the belt of trees seen ahead on the near skyline.

Forge Valley

▶ Turn left on an unmetalled farm lane and walk towards a group of farm buildings.

3 The tree-covered walls of Skell Dikes are the remains of a prehistoric boundary.

▶ As the lane nears the farm buildings take the signposted bridleway on the right.

▶ Go through a gate and turn left to head towards woodland. Turn right after entering the woodland and follow the path, descending down to the car park.

River Derwent

❝ A walk of contrasts and ever-changing views, following a series of forest tracks and visiting two of the most attractive side valleys in the upper Derwent **❞**

Quite often a romantically sounding place name can prove to be a disappointment and anyone visiting this area for the first time can be excused a passing cynicism at the name Whisper Dales. However, here the name fits the situation and Whisper Dales once discovered remains as a pleasurable memory for a long time. The road from Scarborough follows the edge of a north-east-facing escarpment where the gentle southwest slopes are clothed in plantations of mixed conifers. Deep valleys bite into the escarpment, and farms make the most of the shelter offered by forest and a sunny aspect. The ambience of silent forest and farmland is, with the exception of the architecture, reminiscent of the Black Forest in Germany.

View from Reasty Hill Top

Reasty Bank & Whisper Dales

Whisper Dales

Plan your walk

Hartlepool

Middlesbrough

Whitby

Scarborough

Thirsk

Pickering

Norton

York

Selby   Beverley

DISTANCE: 4 miles (6km)

TIME: 2 hours

START/END: SE964944

TERRAIN: Easy; one short uphill section

MAPS:
OS Explorer OL 27;
OS Landranger 101

Route instructions

1 From the car park on Reasty Bank the view northwards is of the upper reaches of the Derwent valley, with tantalising glimpses of the vast expanse of Fylingdales Moor, appearing between the arms of Harwood Dale and Langdale Forests. Wildlife in Broxa Forest includes many woodland species such as roe deer, green woodpeckers and colonies of wood ants. Waymarked Forest Trails start from Reasty Bank, and a complex network of forest roads and firebreaks making it possible to wander for hours on end with only birdsong and the scent of pines for company.

A From the car park cross the road to follow the gravel track opposite, downhill through the forest.

2 The beauty of Whisper Dales comes as a surprise view where the track leaves the forest.

B Beyond the farmhouse, follow the right bank of the stream by a track.

C Cross over to the left bank by the cart bridge and continue downstream through meadowland for 1 mile (1.6km).

D Pass the farm and go over the shallow fords by footbridges. Turn right, walk uphill along a sunken farm lane with flower-bedecked

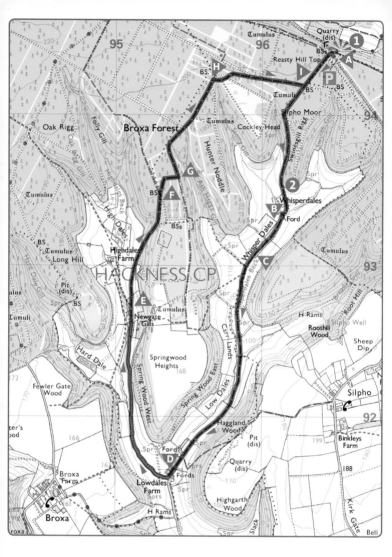

hedgerows for just under 1 mile (1.6km).

E Beyond a pair of red roofed cottages and before the locked metal farm gate, a signpost points to the right diagonally uphill. Follow this direction on a path climbing up to, then through, a plantation of mature pines. The track is steep in places and muddy after rain.

Reasty Bank & Whisper Dales

F At the top of the incline, in a forest clearing, take the right hand fork.

G Turn left on to a gravel-surfaced forest drive.

H Turn right at the second turning on the right. The track follows a more or less level route around the head of the deep-cut Stony Gill.

I Turn left at the pole barrier to rejoin the outward route back to the car park.

Broxa Forest

Whisper Dales

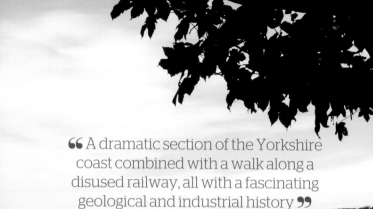

> **❝** A dramatic section of the Yorkshire coast combined with a walk along a disused railway, all with a fascinating geological and industrial history **❞**

Visitors to Ravenscar, known locally as 'Bay Town', can be forgiven if they note a certain unfinished atmosphere about the place. This is because Ravenscar is a holiday resort that began as a speculative venture and was never quite finished. Once there were grandiose ideas of building another Scarborough here, but the unstable geology of the area and the resulting undermining of the sea cliffs made large-scale building a hazardous proposition.

This is an area of complex geology, mostly from the Jurassic Period of about 160 million years ago. Numerous fault lines and weak strata have left the surrounding land and coast in a state of constant flux. As you walk along the bed of the abandoned Yorkshire Coast Railway you will be conscious of this movement, which shows itself prominently in sudden slopes, far steeper than any track gradient.

Ravenscar

Ravenscar

Route instructions

Plan your walk

Hartlepool

Middlesbrough

Whitby

Scarborough

Thirsk

Pickering

Norton

York

Selby

Beverley

DISTANCE: 5 miles (8km)

TIME: 3 hours

START/END: NZ980015

TERRAIN: Moderate; muddy and slippery sections

MAPS:
OS Explorer OL 27;
OS Landranger 94

1 Ravenscar has a seasonal café, The Ravenscar Tea Rooms, as well as the Raven Hall Hotel, a building of some architectural merit. From 1774 it was a private residence and George III was often sent here for treatment during his bouts of madness. In the early 1800s large sums were spent on extending the hall, and the terraced gardens were extended to their present proportions. The hotel is built on the site of a former Roman lookout and signalling station, part of a chain of signal stations built along the coast to warn of attack from the north and east.

A Park along the roadside or in the official car park and leave Ravenscar village by walking down the lane in front of the National Trust Visitor Centre.

2 The National Trust's Ravenscar Coastal Centre provides information on the interesting industrial archaeology of this area. Inland and to the west of the village there is an extensive area of overgrown quarries. Starting in the early part of the 17th century, vast quantities of alum were quarried and processed by a rather unsavoury alchemy requiring the import of urine collected from the inns and public houses of London. Boats carrying the barrelled urine would beach themselves in partially made havens below the cliffs and load up with finished alum

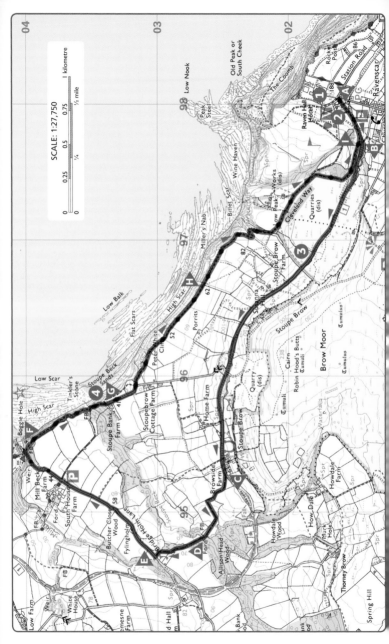

Ravenscar

to sail away on the next high tide. Alum was used as a mordant to 'fix' dyes in woollen cloth. The industry, which ran until about 1871, was started on the instructions of Henry VIII, who wished to break the then papal monopoly of its use in fixing fashionable 'turkey red' dyes. In the early 20th century shale which covered the alum layers, was used for brick-making. Traces of the brick kilns are the only tangible remains of what were once intensively worked quarries.

B Fork left on to the track bed of the old railway line. Follow the railway for about 2 miles (3km) to Browside Farm.

3 Note the evidence of earth movement from the unnatural steepening of the track bed or slumping of land in the fields below and to the right of the railway. Before it closed in 1965 the Yorkshire Coast Railway could boast of being one of the most attractive lines in the North of England.

C Leave the track by a gate on the right, opposite the farm and riding school. Walk downhill through meadowland along a bridleway. Take care here in the wet.

D Cross the stream at the footbridge and climb uphill through a narrow belt of trees.

E Turn right along the road and follow it to the sea at Boggle Hole.

F Turn right to follow the signposted Cleveland Way cliff path away from the sea. Much of the path is sheltered by furze and blackthorn bushes, sometimes a hazard, but a blessing in stormy weather. This section is very slippery when wet.

4 Stoupe Beck Sands is an ideal place for a picnic, either on the beach or foreshore. Difficult road access makes this a very secluded beach.

G Follow the access road above the beach as far as the bend below the second farm (Stoupebrow Cottage Farm). Turn left, back towards the coast as indicated by the Cleveland Way signpost. Follow the cliff path to the right and in the direction of Ravenscar, which should be seen rising prominently ahead.

H Continue following signs for the Cleveland Way, walking away from the coast, uphill towards Ravenscar.

I Turn left on the track which will lead back to Ravenscar.

Brow Moor

66 Walk along the cliff top or take time to explore the shore between the picturesque fishing village of Robin Hood's Bay and the old smugglers cove of Boggle Hole 99

Ever since people have lived in Robin Hood's Bay, they have had the sea as both friend and foe. Fishing as a full-time occupation is a shadow of its former self, when every able-bodied man in this village earned his living from the sea. Open to the ravages of storm-pressed seas, the coast has seen many tragedies, but none more horrific than the wrecking of the hospital ship *Rohilla* in 1914, which ran aground between Whitby and Robin Hood's Bay. As well as shipwrecks, houses have been known to disappear during storms when the soft boulder clay of the cliffs is undermined by wave action. Expensive sea defence schemes can only hope to hold back the remorseless attack of the waves for a comparatively short time.

Robin Hood's Bay

View towards Ravenscar

Route instructions

A Cars must be left at one of the two main car parks and the village approached on foot. Walk downhill towards the beach.

1 Known as the Clovelly of the North, the old part of Robin Hood's Bay can only be approached on foot. Red-roofed houses crowd each other in a picturesque jumble; a jumble, so local legend has it, caused by newly wed couples never wanting to live far from their parents! All the houses have steep staircases and many have a tiny landing window, said to be designed to allow coffins to be lowered into the street.

Spend time exploring the quaint narrow alleys lined with fishermen's cottages. There is no harbour here and boats are launched from the beach or from the main street at high tide. At other stages of the tide fishermen use the shelter of the exposed seaward-curving arms of rock known locally as scars.

2 If the tide is going out, and you allow plenty of time, you can walk along the beach parallel to the cliff as far as Boggle Hole. Time can then be spent looking in pools left by the outgoing tide, or searching for fossils in the rock debris at the base of the cliffs. It may be possible to find ammonites but you will be very lucky to find any of the now-rare jet, a form of fossilised wood.

Plan your walk

Hartlepool
Middlesbrough
Whitby
Scarborough
Thirsk
Pickering
Norton
York
Selby
Beverley

DISTANCE: 2½ miles (4km)

TIME: 2 hours

START/END: NZ950055

TERRAIN: Moderate

MAPS:
OS Explorer OL 27;
OS Landranger 94

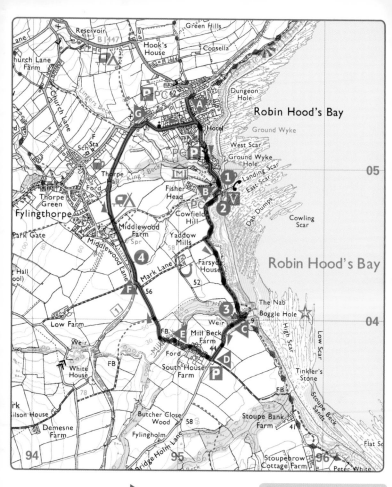

B If the tide is a long way out turn right and walk along the beach, otherwise if the tide is in or coming in, then climb the steps on the right at the bottom of the main street (signposted Cleveland Way). Follow the narrow path along the cliff top.

C Turn right at Boggle Hole and walk inland along the tree-lined lane.

3 Boggle Hole was once a notorious smugglers' haunt. The mill, now converted into a youth hostel, ground flour for 250 years and was powered by Mill Beck. Ships laden with grain arrived at Boggle Hole and had to be pulled up the beck. A 'boggle' is a Yorkshire name for a sprite or hobgoblin who would help people when treated kindly enough.

Robin Hood's Bay

D Turn right between a group of farm buildings then through the farmyard and follow the lane downhill.

E Follow the road across the valley, crossing Mill Beck by the footbridge, and climb the hawthorn-lined lane up to the tarmac road.

F Leave the road by turning right to climb the disused railway embankment up onto the track. Then follow it as far as Robin Hood's Bay

4 This route follows the track bed of the former Scarborough to Whitby railway line which ran from 1885 until its closure in 1965.

G Leave the railway track where it joins the road and turn right to return to the starting point.

Robin Hood's Bay

&& A justifiably popular town and resort, this walk reveals much of historical Whitby **99**

The long march of history has left its indelible mark on Whitby. The street patterns around the harbour would be recognisable even today to Captain Cook, whose locally built *Endeavour* took him on his voyages of discovery.

Whitby reached its zenith as a port in the heyday of whaling and many fine Regency buildings above the west town speak of the wealth created from this barbaric industry.

If you can ignore the candy floss of West Shore and explore the byways of this fascinating town, it will become a journey of discovery where tantalising links with the past are found around almost every corner. On a damp misty day visions of Bram Stoker's Dracula may lurk near the sombre tombstones on top of East Cliff.

Whitby harbour

Whitby

Whitby Abbey ruins

Plan your walk

DISTANCE: 2½ miles (4km)

TIME: 1½ hours

START/END: NZ900113

TERRAIN: Easy

MAPS:
OS Explorer OL 27;
OS Landranger 94

Route instructions

A Start the walk by climbing the 199 steps from the Old Town to Whitby's Church of St Mary.

1 An intricately carved memorial column at the top of the steps is to Caedmon, a medieval monk from nearby St Hilda's Abbey, whose *Song of Creation* is the earliest known religious poem in English literature. The exterior of St Mary's Church, dating from 1110, has been modified but its interior is unique. The panelling and box pews date from the 17th and 18th centuries. The Chomley family pew with its barley-sugar-twist is interesting.

B At the top of the steps go straight through the churchyard, exiting through the large gateposts at the top. Follow the road around the abbey perimeter wall in a sweeping right hand curve.

2 St Hilda founded Whitby Abbey in AD 657. She was the daughter of a king of Northumberland and her abbey, which housed both monks and nuns, grew over the centuries into its present but ruined state. Abandoned after the dissolution of the monasteries in 1593, it suffered further damage in 1914 during the bombardment of the town by a German cruiser.

C At the end of the grassed area, turn left at the Cleveland Way signpost

walk 19 Whitby **89**

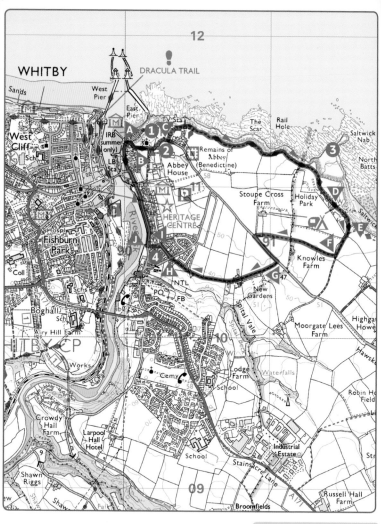

passing the farm buildings as far as a gate. Turn right here and follow the cliff-top path.

3 The view of Saltwick Nab is in dramatic contrast to bustling Whitby. The headland is a jumble

of sedimentary rocks overlooking Saltwick Bay, where the hospital ship *Rohilla* ran aground in 1914.

D Walk through the holiday park, following the Cleveland Way signs,

Whitby

out along its access drive.

E Turn right on to a metalled lane.

F Leave the lane at a footpath into the near corner of the third field on the right beyond the holiday park. Cross a series of fields (may be muddy when wet) as far as the road. Turn left at the road.

G Follow the road for about a quarter of a mile (200m) then turn right onto a footpath towards a farm. Go through the farmyard on to the farm lane.

H Where the farm lane turns right, walk ahead on a flagged path into the outskirts of Whitby.

I Pass the old hospital building and turn left down a stepped alley.

4 Salt Pan Steps is one of many old ways out of the town.

J Turn right along the inner harbour towards Whitby town centre.

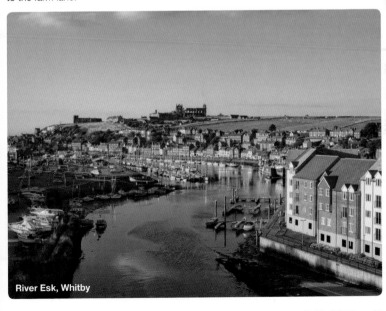

River Esk, Whitby

" This walk explores the fishing village of Staithes, then follows the coast as far as Port Mulgrave before turning inland to the wooded shelter of Borrowby Dale "

Staithes likes to claim Captain Cook as its own, but he was not born in Staithes and neither did he study seamanship here. He was apprenticed to a local draper and the germ of his ambition to become a navigator probably came to the young James Cook as he watched the fishing cobles sail in and out of the harbour which was then open to the ravages of the North Sea.

Staithes harbour

Staithes

Staithes

Plan your walk

Hartlepool
Middlesbrough
Whitby
Scarborough
Thirsk
Pickering
Norton
York
Selby
Beverley

DISTANCE: 4 miles (6.5km)

TIME: 2 hours

START/END: NZ781185

TERRAIN: Easy; muddy on woodland section when wet

MAPS:
OS Explorer OL 27;
OS Landranger 94

Route instructions

A Leave your car at the old railway car park. Walk down the hill into the lower and oldest part of Staithes.

1 Allow plenty of time to explore this quaint fishing village; one of the best vantage points is from the outer harbour wall. Access is by way of the beach beneath Cowbar Nab, so make sure the incoming tide does not cut you off.

Houses along the harbour side were frequently wrecked; the cosy Cod and Lobster public house, the closest remaining building to the harbour, has had to be rebuilt many times.

The design of fishing boats on this exposed coast

evolved from the Viking Longships, which came to the north-east coast looking for easy pickings. Known locally as 'cobles', they are broad amidships high in both bow and stern, and able to ride the steep inshore surf.

B Leave the village by the narrow street on the right beyond the Cod and Lobster. Pass the house which claims to be where Cook lived and follow the coast path up the cliff by way of a series of steps. Go past the farm and then out on to open fields for a little over 1 mile (1.6km).

2 Viewpoint of Port Mulgrave, which is now almost silted up, but was

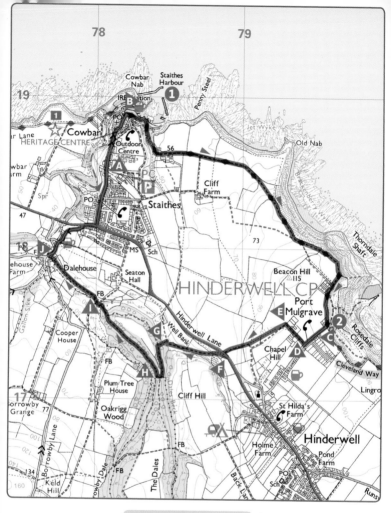

once a busy harbour. Iron-ore was brought along a tunnel on a narrow gauge railway from mines around Boulby.

C Bear right and follow the road away from the sea.

D Turn right opposite a telephone box into the

lane between two substantially built houses, one time homes of harbour officials.

E Bear left beyond the houses and cross three fields. When the A174 comes into view, walk to the right of the final field boundary.

Staithes

F Cross the A174 and head towards the slip road then down some steps. Follow the path down into the wooded valley.

G Cross Dales Beck by a footbridge, then follow the path uphill and to the left.

H Turn right at the junction of paths and walk to a gate at the end of the wood. Walk along the long, narrow field and go through a belt of trees. The track now descends steeply towards a wooden bridge by the caravan site.

I Cross the bridge and follow the caravan access lane as far as the side road.

J Turn right at the road and follow it as far as the main A174. Cross over and turn left into Staithes.

Staithes harbour

Photo credits

All photographs © HarperCollins Publishers Ltd,
photographer Alex Wallace, with the exception of:

Page 4: © HarperCollins Publishers,
photographer Sonia Dawkins

Page 12: © sepavo /
Shutterstock images

Page 16: © HarperCollins Publishers,
photographer Sonia Dawkins

Page 17: © HarperCollins Publishers,
photographer Sonia Dawkins

Page 19: © HarperCollins Publishers,
photographer Sonia Dawkins

Page 20: © David Robertson / Alamy

Page 24: © Gary Stephenson / Alamy

Page 28: © funkyfood London –
Paul Williams / Alamy

Page 32: © Mike Kipling / Alamy

Page 36: © JCElv / Shutterstock images

Page 40: © Kevin Eaves /
Shutterstock images

Page 41: © Kevin Eaves /
Shutterstock images

Page 43: © Kevin Eaves /
Shutterstock images

Page 44: © Captured Sight / Alamy

Page 48: © John Devlin / Alamy

Page 52: © Joss Smithson / (CC by sa 2.0)

Page 56: © Mike Kipling / Alamy

Page 60: © KAppleyard /
Shutterstock images

Page 64: © Mike Kipling / Alamy

Page 68: © Kevin Eaves /
Shutterstock images

Page 72: © Tom Curtis /
Shutterstock images

Page 76: © Mike Kipling / Alamy

Page 80: © Tom Curtis /
Shutterstock images

Page 81: © Tom Curtis /
Shutterstock images

Page 84: © Kevin Eaves /
Shutterstock images

Page 88: © Quayside /
Shutterstock images

Page 91: © Kevin Eaves /
Shutterstock images

Page 92: © Kevin Eaves /
Shutterstock images

Page 93: © Gordon Bell /
Shutterstock images

Page 95: © Kevin Eaves /
Shutterstock images